Dogs can't Read

WHY WE LEARN TO READ

BY MARIA GORDON
ILLUSTRATED BY MIKE GORDON

WAYLAND

Titles in the series:
Dogs can't Read
Mice can't Write
Cats can't Count
Spiders can't Spell

HOW TO USE THIS BOOK:

Children will enjoy reading the words and looking at the pictures together with an adult. At the same time, children can discover the uses and advantages of reading. Used in combination with the activities at the end of the book, the suggestions will generate lots of fun and reading.

All Wayland books encourage children to read and help them improve their literacy.

Series editor: Sarah Doughty
Book editor: Liz Harman
Cover design: Giles Wheeler/Malcolm Walker
Inside design: Malcolm Walker
Consultant: Roy Blatchford

This edition published in 1999 by Wayland Publishers Ltd
61 Western Road, Hove, East Sussex, BN3 1JD, England

British Library Cataloguing in Publication Data
Gordon, Maria
Dogs can't read: why we learn to read. – (Animals can't)
1. Books and reading – Juvenile literature
I.Title
428.4

ISBN 0 7502 2483 5

Printed and bound by Edições ASA, Portugal

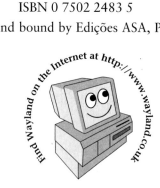

Find Wayland on the Internet at http://www.wayland.co.uk

Author's thanks
The author would like to thank the many bookstore staff, teachers and librarians who gave their valuable assistance. For their generous help and support, Claire Bellanca, Ellen Kindl, and Jim Kornell are warmly appreciated, and Liz Harman deserves a medal in gratitude for all her unstinting effort, time and dedication as editor of the books in this series.

This is Ben.
His dog is called Zak.

Ben can read.
Zak cannot.

Ben gets out his bike.

Ben can read the label.
Zak cannot.

Ben is well.

Zak is not well.

Ben rides his bike.

Ben can read the sign.
Zak cannot.

Ben is safe.

Zak is not safe.

Ben is in the park.

Ben can read the notice.
Zak cannot.

Ben is clean.

Zak is not clean.

Ben rides on the path.

Ben can read the sign.
Zak cannot.

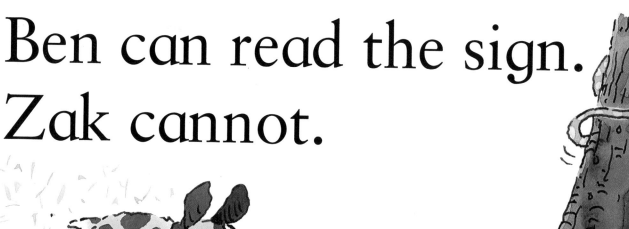

Ben has fun.

keep off

Zak does not have fun.

Ben visits his grandad.

Ben can read the notice.
Zak cannot.

Ben gets into the house.

Zak does not get in.

Ben and Grandad go to
the museum.

Ben can read the sign.
Zak cannot.

Ben knows the way.

Zak does not know the way.

Ben and Grandad go in the lift.

Ben can read the words.
Zak cannot.

Ben and Grandad go up.

Zak does not go up.

Ben and Grandad are going home.

Ben can read the sign.
Zak cannot.

Ben and Grandad go down.

Zak does not go down.

Ben is hungry.

Ben can read
the buttons.
Zak cannot.

Ben has a snack.

Zak does not have a snack.

Ben and Grandad cross the street.

Ben can read the sign.
Zak cannot.

Ben is safe.

Zak is not safe.

Ben and Grandad go home.

Ben can read
the newspaper.
Zak cannot.

24

Ben is warm.

Zak is not warm.

Ben is upstairs.

Ben can read the notice.
Zak cannot.

Ben is quiet.

Zak is
not quiet.

Grandad has gifts for
Ben and Zak.

Ben can read the names.
Zak cannot.

Ben has fun with his gift.

Zak does too!

Notes for Adults

Lucky children associate reading with closeness, comfort and fun from an early age. This is a foundation to build on by showing how reading is vital to our everyday world. Actual experience teaches the way reading warns, instructs, directs and informs as well as entertains. This book provides entertaining examples of some of the uses of reading in life.

The short sentences, elementary vocabulary and repetition used in the text all contribute to helping young readers to develop reading skills, while the illustrations support and enlarge the story.

The notes that follow expand on the ideas contained in the story, and suggest activities to help you make reading and its skills relevant and enjoyable for young children in their everyday lives. Each child will benefit from attention and praise of his or her reading skills and effort.

The Word Hunt is an activity designed to encourage children to review material and to practise skills basic to the use of indexes and glossaries. Learning to put words into alphabetical order increases knowledge of the individual letters as well as aiding the search for information in books, directories or on the Internet. All these skills, in turn, help to enhance literacy by increasing fluency and vocabulary.

Activities

Word Hunt

Use this Word Hunt (see panel below) to turn the story into a reading skills game. Ask children to read the words in the box below and to find them in the story, noting down the numbers of the page(s) on which each word appears. Help the children to put all the words they have found into alphabetical order. You could write them on cards and ask the children to rearrange them.

You could also use the key words from the Word Hunt to make a word search by 'hiding' some of the keywords in a letter-filled grid of 10 x 10 squares.

• Re-read page 3. Ask 'Who do you know who can read?'. Be sure children include themselves. Find or discuss some of the places where you might see people's or pets' names written, for example, name tags (see page 3), badges (see page 3), signs on doors, gift tags (see page 28), letters, sports kit or school uniform and even car number plates. Pin up giant capital letters; have children add the rest of the letters of their name, and the names of friends and relatives next to the correct capital letter.

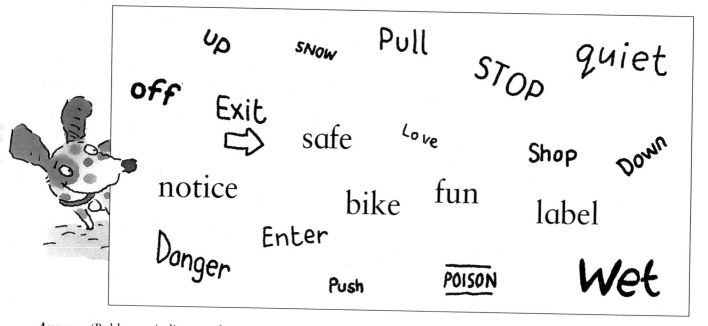

Answers (Bold type indicates where words appear in the illustrations): bike p.4 & 6; danger p.6; down p.18 & 19/**19**; enter p.**14**; exit p.**15**; fun p.11 & 29; label p.**4**; love p.28; notice p.8, 12 & 26; off p.**10** & **11**; poison p.4 & 5; pull p.**12** & **13**; push p.**20**; quiet p.**26** & **27**; safe p.7 & 23; shop p.**17**; snow p. 24; stop p.**22** & **23**; up p.**16**, **17** & **19**; wet p.**8** & **9**.

• Discuss some of the warning words in the story – 'poison' (pages 4 and 5), 'danger' (page 6), 'keep off' (pages 10 and 11), 'wet paint' (pages 8 and 9), 'stop' (pages 22 and 23). What other words do we often see that help to keep us safe? When visiting a public place such as a museum, station, cinema, etc., encourage children to notice written signs, particularly those relating to safety (e.g. fire escape, emergency exit, no entry, danger, etc.). Look at warning labels on cleaning or gardening products and encourage children to notice use of colour and symbols, such as the skull and crossbones symbol used on poisons (see pages 4 and 5). Are specific colours associated with warning signs? For example, discuss how red can signify 'stop', 'hot' or a different type of warning (see pages 6, 7, 22 and 23).

• Use CVC (consonant-vowel-consonant) words from the text (e.g. wet, can, Ben, dog, his, not, has, fun, etc.) to create lists of rhyming words by changing the first letter each time, for example: wet – get, met, pet, let, bet. Can children spot an odd word out? (e.g. web, bet, pot)? Encourage children to make up rhymes (e.g. 'I let my pet get wet.'). Explore making new words by changing the end consonant of CVC words, for example: can – cab, can, cap, car, cat, and changing the vowel, for example: Ben – ban, bin, bun. Have fun making up nonsense CVC words!

• Use phonics, splitting simple words into separate parts, each part having a separate sound. These words can include objects like 'dog' (d-og), 'label' (la-bel), 'snack' (sn-ack) and actions such as 'push' (p-ush), 'press' (pr-ess), 'lift' (lif-t) and 'open' (o-pen). Write each part of the word on a card or square of paper and ask children to select and order the correct sounds to make each word. Add a new activity by writing the words on labels for children to attach to appropriate objects (e.g. 'snack' on an apple, 'open' on a door), and inappropriate ones, too, for fun (e.g. 'snack' on a dog)!

• Ask children to find words that have the same letter combinations, for example, 'read', 'beak' and 'meat', or 'house', 'mouth', 'out'. Show how different combinations can make the same sounds, for example, 'street' and 'feet' share the same middle sound as 'read' and 'bead'. Once children can easily recognize and read different combinations, show how some combinations can make different sounds, e.g. 'book', 'foot' and 'boot', 'loose'. Use 'down' (pages 16–19) as a major example. Stress the 'ow' sound and encourage children to think of rhymes (e.g. 'brown', 'gown', 'crown').

Write 'ow' on a card and place it in gaps between letters like t_ _n, fr_ _n, cl_ _n, etc. As a separate task, work with 'ow' as a long vowel sound, as in 'snow', 'slow', 'flow', 'blow', 'grow', etc.

• What makes 'quiet' (page 26), 'sign' (pages 3, 10, 14, 18 and 22), 'poison' (pages 4 and 5), 'house' (page 13) and 'know' (page 15) hard words to read? Look at common sight-recognition words, which cannot be read by sounding out the letters (e.g. laugh, love, night, people). Write some of these words on cards and pin up pictures that illustrate them. Ask children to match the cards to the pictures. Point out the hard words 'Wednesday' and 'Tuesday' on newspapers and calendars. Write out the prefixes of the seven day names on cards and write the suffix 'day' on another card. Ask children to read which day is being spelled as you hold up a different prefix next to the suffix. Many numbers (e.g. two, three) are also hard to read at first. Encourage children to practise reading these. Ask them to choose the correct numbers, written on cards, to place beside groups of different numbers of objects, such as three apples, five books, ten pencils, etc.

• At the end of the story, Grandad gives Ben a book as a gift (see pages 28–9). Talk about what books are for. Encourage children to think of something that they have learned from a book. What is their favourite storybook? What books might a dog like to read? What is an author, an illustrator, etc? Where are the capital letters? From which side do we start reading the lines? Find examples of text from other cultures that are read in different directions.

• What other forms of reading material can children think of besides books? (e.g. letters, food labels, newspapers/magazines/comics, text on computers, street signs, badges, etc.). Cut out samples of words in a wide range of different styles and typefaces and discuss them. If possible, provide samples of Braille for children to feel, and make Braille-type cards with letter shapes punched through in mirror image with a pin.

• What sort of words would an alien see if it crash-landed in a town, in the country, by a school or by a shop? If the alien decided to live in a town, when would it need to read? (e.g. shopping, driving, using a computer, phoning home, etc.).

Recommended reading

Maisie's ABC by Lucy Cousins (Walker, 1994)
Maisie is a mouse, joined by her friends in a colourful, simple, lift-the-flap progression with amusing text.

Each Peach, Pear, Plum by Janet & Allan Ahlberg (Penguin, 1989)
A picture book with enjoyable rhyming text based on well-known characters who adventure beyond their normal fairytales and nursery rhymes. Humorous illustrations and excellent involvement for readers.

I Like Books by Anthony Browne (Walker, 1994)
A picture book where the central character, Willy, explores all sorts of different types of books – such as fat books, thin books and big books and finds that he likes them all. An appreciation of reading in its different formats for the very young.

The Orchard ABC by Ian Beck (Orchard Books, 1994)
Each letter tells a story in this book of favourite tales. An aid for teaching the alphabet.

Can't You Sleep, Little Bear? by Martin Waddell and Barbara Firth (Walker, 1998)
Big Bear reassures Little Bear when he can't get to sleep, allaying fears of the dark that are shared among many children. Big Bear is a lovely role model of a persistent reader!

Resources for adults

The Reading is Fundamental Family Guide to Encouraging Young Readers (Scholastic)

Beginning with Books (Book Trust, Scotland)

Reading Together Parents' Handbook (Walker Books)

Read and Write Together (Basic Skills Agency)

Useful addresses

The Basic Skills Agency is an excellent source of support material for parents and teachers involved in teaching reading, writing and arithmetic. They can be contacted at:

Commonwealth House, 1–19 New Oxford Street, London WC1A 1NU
Tel. 0171 405 4017   Fax. 0171 440 6626

Reading is Fundamental, UK is a charitable organization that helps children grow up with a love of books and reading. It gives practical help to parents in becoming involved with their children's reading.

They can be contacted at:
The National Literacy Trust, Swire House, London SW1E 6AJ
Tel. 0171 828 2435 Fax. 0171 931 9986

Book Trust is a charity which promotes the book, and manages books for the babies project known as Bookstart. They can be contacted at:

Book House, 45 East Hill, Wandsworth, London SW18 2QZ
Tel. 0181 516 2977 Fax. 0181 516 2978